Where hazel falls

AN ANTHOLOGY OF MODERN IRISH VERSE

electric
publications

First edition published 2006 by
Electric Publications,
71 Main Street, Gorey,
Co. Wexford, Ireland.
www.electricpublications.com

ISBN 0955060710

A CIP catalogue record for this book is available from the British Library.

Set in 10 point Frutiger Light. Printed and typeset in Ireland by Electric Design, Co. Wexford (www.electricdesign.ie). Bound by Print Finishers Ltd, Dublin.

Printed on 100% recycled paper

Contents

"Sinend, daughter of Lodan Lucharglan son of Ler out of Tir Tairngire (Land of Promise, Fairyland), went to Connla's Well, which is under sea, to behold it. That is a well at which are the hazels and inspirations of wisdom, that is, the hazels of the science of poetry, and in the same hour their fruit and their blossom and their foliage break forth, and these fall on the well in the same shower, which raises on the water a royal surge of purple. Then the salmon chew the fruit, and the juice of the nuts is apparent on their purple beffies. And 'Seven Streams of Wisdom' spring forth and turn there again."

From Whitely Stokes' translation of the Connla legend,
Revue Celtique, xv. 457 (1894)

Introduction

You might be forgiven for thinking that poetry is a dying art in Ireland, what with the ubiquitous reality television, myriad magazines, game consoles and four-wheel drives to distract us from older cultural activities. You might be forgiven for thinking the art of conversation is dead, traditional music is silenced and the poet, formerly much loved in Ireland, has become mute.

What has surprised me, is not the demise of these great art forms but their strength and endurance against a backdrop of modernity. In the case of poetry, the country, it seems, is overflowing with poets. A short run of Toddy Kennedy's first collection *Introduction* was lapped up like hot cakes, leading to second and third runs of the same which prompted us to consider poetry on a wider scale.

The moment the seed of that idea was planted, no end of poets began to appear out of the woodwork. To my great pleasure and amazement nine poets of merit found their way to my desk without one single notice or advertisement, which for a small and almost unknown publisher is quite incredible.

This collection features poets of greatly varying age and background, with differing styles and interests and that is reflected in their work. What strikes me most about this collection is the connection to this land that is evident as a common thread running through this book.

Perhaps in these times of economic expansion, mass development and cultural change we need to listen to the voice of the poet even more than in former times. In this age of lightning fast communication, how much of it is really saying anything? Amidst the stress and logic of modern life there has to be room for reflection and appreciation of all that is good and bad in life; and I believe that poetry is as relevant to the understanding of the human condition now as it has ever been.

L. Eastwood, Editor

Ann Dalton

Ann Dalton has recently returned to her native Cork, having lived in London for over 10 years. She first started 'exposing' the poetry she had written when she discovered London's poetry performance circuit in the early 1990's. During this period she co-ran a poetry and acoustic music club in North London and, in collaboration with 3 other artists, produced a CD of poetry and music called *Freshtracks*. Her poems have been displayed on London Buses and included in a anthology of poetry by Irish women living in London, published by *Survivors Poetry Press*. She continues to write and is delighted to be part of this new collection.

July Lady

Count the lilac trees in London in July,
In the gardens while you walk by on the street,
While you pass by on the bus
Or on the back of someone's bike.

Count the little girls in lilac dresses in London in July,
In the parks or in the playground
As you pass by in the middle of a crucial decision.
Count the women wearing lilac lipstick in London in July,
On the underground
While you remember that you're not in love
And wonder if you are in fashion,
As you sit there in your blue dress and pink lipstick.

Last Summer you were someone's July lady,
And you can't recall what colour was in fashion,
But who cares when you're in love,
You throw all colours in the face of fashion
And say 'Heh',
'You could never be in love like me!'

In love, out of fashion,
Out of love, back in fashion,
In fashion, out of love,
Back in love, out of fashion.

It's July in London
And you're not in love.
Perhaps you should wear lilac lipstick
And count the lilac trees by day
And by night dream of Springtime,
When yellow might be the colour,
But you might be in love and count daffodils
And wear bright orange
Just to be out of fashion.

Sparkle

I have a feeling that I know what you're feeling,
A closed red door
With a sign that says 'no smoking',
A man alone on a naked stage
Makes my heart stop beating
Momentarily
A single chord
Tells me you are leaving.

Writing words without a pen,
Keeps my heart invisible,
From those who rip my belly open,
Only wanting caviar.
While others who are keen observers,
Stand right back and read these eyes
That cry out in the faintest whisper
'I have a feeling…

An Irish Mother

Someday I'd like to be and Irish mother,
As fast as a March hare,
As daft as any poet's dream,
As musical as the tunes in my memory
And as witty as *I'd* like to be.

Oh, wouldn't it be wonderful
To have a boy or girl,
Who one day would wax lyrical
(*About me*)...

Oh, you should have known my mother,
She was as quick as lightening,
And said she could see the wind.
She was mad in a way that would make
Any child proud,
She had a song to match each moment
Of my childhood days
And she could outwit *even me*!

Different Tribes

At first, I didn't notice the colour of your skin,
All I could see was the glow of your heart from within.
To begin with I didn't question what you did or didn't believe in,
Your capacity to love seemed all that was needed.

At first when I traveled I didn't realise
That the world just got bigger and bigger,
The more places I visited,
The more people I met,
The more knowledge I gained,
The more open-minded I became,
The more experiences I encountered,
The more lines that were carved in my skin.

The closer I got to you,
The more I knew,
The less I understood,
The more complex life grew,
The more I questioned the time
When I had been narrow-minded,
Held back in blindness
And I listened when they told me
'To try a little kindness',
And we did....

But you are not I
And I am not you,
Yet together, we are 'you and I',
But you and I are different in body and mind
And we have opened up so much,
We are trapped inside,
Trapped inside the narrow corridors of other minds.

Does the butterfly think itself wise,
To come outside in its colour and splendour
And fly from flower to flower?
Was it not safe until it became beautiful
And grew its wings?

When we rush out to view the comet,
We take all the stars for granted
And neglect those that shine for us every night.
When we memorise the words of our favourite song,
We immediately lose part of its meaning,
We just sing along,
Just sing along,
Just sing along.

When we first feel the flow of the river,
We don't anticipate its twists and turns,
We just go with the flow,
Go with the flow,
Go with the flow....

Until our open minds are capsized
And we are sucked into the currents
Of different tribes,
Different tribes,
Different tribes.

Poem for Sam

I am the princess of the countryside,
All eyes gaze upon me
As I pass by fields of Autumn green,
Bedecked with blackberry bushes,
Ripening for their princess.

No face will turn away
Until I am less than a (royal) dot
On the horizon.
Not 'til then
And only then,
Will the silent reverence
Be interrupted by the munching
On a blade of grass.

Happy New Year Sadness

I stop to listen to the busker,
His fancy Spanish style keeps me standing in the cold
A little longer than I'd planned on New Year's day.
But then, that's why I'm here,
To soak up a little of the atmosphere,
What better place than on the piazza
With a small crowd gathering
And the evening closing in.

But this event was never meant to be a simple pleasure,
For I find I've stood beside a drunkard,
Who immediately has planned to be my friend.
And so I go along with it,
After all, it's New Year's day
And, besides I have to say
That he was far too big
To consider making him my enemy.

He tried to share the music with me,
But his speech was incoherent
And his nose had the appearance
Of one who'd met
Too many fists along the way.
But each time he pointed at the busker,
His eyes lit up like the millennium fireworks
And then I knew what he was trying to say.

'This music fills my soul,
Keeps me warm out in the cold,
Makes me part of this big crowd
Not just an outsider.
And if it wasn't for these notes,
You and I might not have thought
That we could ever connect
Here on the Piazza'.

I want to reply and say
'Please take your eyes away,
For although I share your happiness
I also see,
That this music here today
Has but drawn a bucketful of joy
From a well that's mostly filled
With deep deep sadness.'

But instead I wish him A Happy New Year
As he kisses my hand like an old gentleman
And his eyes well up with tears
As do mine.
I walk away and hope
That the music can lift him up
In bucketfuls of joy again and again.

And in our lives we tread
That fine line between sorrow and joy,
And stumble from a smile to a heavy heart.
And if we are blessed, we trundle along
And keep hearing these musical notes,
On the piazza, in the gutter, everywhere.

Musical notes

Silhouettes of buttered *blues*
and *crimson* clouds of poppy flower tunes.
Turquoise stones that roll around
and knock the *pink* right out of sound.

Music dancing through the colour spectrum
along with life and memories of me and you.

And what the history books try their hardest to conceal
is all recorded onto vinyl, tape and digital.

Godchild

I want to be a snowflake
Soothing the insane.
I want to be the sunshine
Penetrating pain.
I want to be a mountain
Sheltering the lonely.
I want to be the still green valley
Welcoming and homely.

So...........
Each time you see a snowflake
Laugh at your insanity.
Each time the sun shines I will hide
Your pain far from reality.
Each time the mountains rise and fall
You'll not have far to roam.
And when you reach that still green valley
Rejoice, for you are home!

Untitled

Those frightened eyes
They run inside
And lock these images in little cells
And push them around in streams of blue
And they puzzle us when they flow out red
But most of all they puzzle you.

Those frightened eyes
They hide behind
And lock these images in clean white sheets
And lose themselves in little creases.
When ironed out,
It puzzles us their disappearance,
But most of all
It puzzles you.

Those frightened eyes
They roll inside
And lock these images behind closed lids
|And it puzzles us
When they do not open
But no longer does it puzzle you,
No longer does it puzzle you.

The Nightingale

A bird flew out of my window
I watched him escape with my freedom
As he soared into the night sky
Turning my light into darkness.

Where will he go on his journey?
Across some far away ocean.
What if he loses my freedom
Will I find it someday washed up
On the shore?

Will he fly over mountains
And drop it mid-flight on their highest peak.
What if it rolls downhill with the stones
Will I find it someday tumbling into
My valley?

Will he fly over forests
And drop it mid-flight on the tallest of trees.
What if it falls with the chestnuts in Autumn
Will I find it someday beneath the leaves?

Will he fly into the heavens
And drop it mid-flight amid the stars.
What if it lands on the luckiest one
Will I find it someday tumbling from the sky?

Will he return from his journey
And land outside of my window.
What if it's closed and in darkness
Will he wait there 'til dawn
With my freedom?

Ted Sludds

Ted Sludds is a writer of fiction, non-fiction and poetry. His publication credits include *Books Ireland*, *Start Magazine*, *Reach Journal* and *Poetry Ireland Review*. He is a past winner of the Impressions National Poetry Award and the Clogh Writers' Prize.

Hard Love

I'll quicken my pace just to get clear of it all.
Family stuff was never my type of business
and she knew that from the start.
I'm impatient with a temper - a dangerous combination
when you're surrounded by kids all day and
a wife who can't look at you without distain.

It's best all round, I've come to convince myself of that,
though I'm the victim in all of this really.
I wanted the terminations and to keep things open
but she wouldn't hear of it, told me it wasn't love
if we could do it with whoever we wanted,
told me with each new arrival they'd
help cement things between us.
"Cement," now there's a word with love in it.

Mangan Still in Dublin

How shapeless it all seems,
caught fighting to make things clear,
to catch the ear of an echo...

Hearer then of just the word,
lost in the chatter of the everyday,
the voiceless listener, quenched by thirst...

Confused and forgotten,
signature of the solitary figure,
his statue in this public garden,
speaking freely at last...

It's just a car passing

Don't let that noise distract you,
turn around and look at me.

Don't make excuses when we both know the truth,
I've been a bollocks and nothing's going to change that.
I suppose I'm looking for a second chance,
so what that I don't deserve it?

Go then.
You're probably right,
what's the point in pretending anymore.

What, question!

Coloured by the well-forgotten questions,
the parts of who we are that remain unanswered,
the little things that bind us tight together.
Those half-felt feelings that return to bring you close.

What's left, then, after the hardship of breaking free,
the everyday seen from this new place,
not greener or more lovely but still enclosed,
still just our way, our vulgar wishes, our incomprehension.
And if things were different, would we be left guessing?

We the Hermit

Hasten past the hours glow,
the fresh fair of a new beginning,
like Anthony upon a desert dune,
captured by the thought of simple solemnity.

Just woken now, our town looks new,
at five in the morning it still slumbers,
as London did for Woodsworth on Westminster Bridge,
yet not calmly, not the sleep of rejuvenation
but of turmoil, of a hope that comes crashing
'round our feet with alarm bells!
The readymade news and digestible collops of information
lain on our computer screens.

And we the hermit amongst it all,
we the towers and sewers about it,
we the free-floating fear mongers
hard pressed to see meaning in a flower . . .

It's Like it Knows

How it falls . . .
through the ages, quiet,
though not quite silent,
sure of knowing only it has a place,
a rooftop, hedgerow, forest-floor or shipyard.

And over time we've heard it
but always as an intermission,
the confluence of our everyday bafflement -
wedged as ever against our inevitable demise.

Dish Washing

The delph in the sink
reminds me of the old days,
long before we bought the Zanussi,
when being married was something
new for both of us.
Before the children came along,
before we lost sight
of how to talk to one another,
before the doctors gave us the news.
It's just a plate now, a saucer, a cup,
and a memory of old times
that stings with pain.

My Awakening

This blood stained bed is not my own
but soon shall be.
My fight was yours
before it became mine, so close the
end that kept the freedom and the peace.
I lie beneath these
blood stained sheets, fall and slip from
consciousness to wake.

Innocence

When innocence is blamed for silence
and cast aside like trouble,
and facing up to terror is turned to shame
by the virtuous who pride themselves as communicants,
then it's time to go . . .

Incidents remembered two-facedly
as not worth recalling,
time then to recognise the hypocrisy
and cry wolf before they turn to sheep
and escape to blind pastures to lamb again.

Fear finds a shelter in the weak,
ratchets up its dander by turning flea-like in their ear,
combs the sordid strokes of misery into prayer
and makes their lives ever shallower.

They make amends by reciting the sorrow of sorries,
ignore the need for deeds
and lie broken-backed but steely eyed
cornering the market in sincerity,
who'd ever think *they* kept a safe house?

How then to move on and let go?
Patience - take your time to fill the truth,
remember only those things that remain right,
learn to pass without a glance,
and turn before the end to finish.

Look Closely

I see my seeing it as strange -
a bird unable to fly, not broken-winged or a fledging
but just indifferent.

Doleful on his own,
perched in a Foxglove-embroidered hedgerow,
owl-like in his not knowing,
thoughtful in his confusion,
bewildered even, baffled,
tumbling back to earth.

Joseph Dawton

Joseph lives near Bunclody, Co. Wexford; he has a chequered past, having worked in a wide range of jobs from journalist to cark park attendant. Joseph has travelled extensively and followed many religions during his life but has found a spiritual path he feels content with in modern-day Druidry.

He has been writing poetry since his teenage years but this is his first collection to be published. His poetry focuses mainly on the natural world, romance and the bizarre workings of human society. Joseph is also author of the spiritual epistle *The Journey*, also published by Electric Publications.

Rain

A Sunday afternoon, late Spring,
My windscreen smudged with dirt
And tiny droplets of glass.
The faint hum of drilling rain on metal
Accompanies the droning of the radio.

A chilling wind rustles through
A half open window,
Its bitter tang of winter
Yet untamed.

Alone again,
A million mile expanse
Of slick concrete before me,
Hurtling into oblivion
In an iron heap.

I turned off,
And the shimmering tarmac
Lined with green, unfolded,
Meandering through green pastures
Lush with liquid.

I pulled up and got out,
A fine spray fresh upon my face,
Among a leafy world of such freshness
Yet so cruelly scarred
By our very existence.

I looked around:
A stream, beer cans, and a broken bottle;
A poster proclaiming
Two hundred new scars to be gouged
In a face already much scarred.

I tore it down in anger,
Yet what difference can it make?
Aren't we already too deeply ensnared
In our own greed to care?
Too far travelled down this road to turn back?

I turned around,
The rain still beating against my face.
My heart heavy, I drove on
From a place, a beauty
That I would not see again.

When The Clock Strikes

When the clock strikes inside her head
The mask comes down
And the murderer, chained for so long,
Breaks free and bolts his cell;
Rampaging through her mind
Slashing, ripping trearing,
At the thin film of sanity;
Stopping the pendulum in its track
And smashing the balance to the floor,
In a wild, urgent frenzy
The blackest thoughts spring forth.

All inhibition is swept away
In a tidal wave of anarchy
And this evil tumor,
In the very soul of man
Rears it's fearsome head,
Crackling through the frail veneer
Of human kindness.
For ultimately we cannot hide
What is our darker nature
Nor the melancholic chimes
When the demon is awaking.

Why?

Do we live to earn
Or do we earn to live?
Why must our days be filled
With concrete, plastic packaging
And oven-ready, frozen meals?
Is there no place to run
From the pearly-white smiles
Of advertising dreamland?
If life must be this grey
Just what is the point?
What is the fucking point?

A Sanctuary

The sun smiled sweetly upon the valley
Bubbling through the laminated sky,
More clear and blue than
Ever I had seen it;
Like a bright sapphire encasing the Earth.

I walked through village after dreamy village,
The only sounds: the river rolling by,
And the low drone of insects.
Such beauty could not fail to lift my heart,
Such peace fail to move me.

The day unravelled before me,
Its delicate landscape prostrate at my feet
As my tired city senses
Stirred at the marvel of nature's beauty.

The noise, the grime and smoke
Lay far behind me,
Relinquished for a different world,
Bursting with life's gifts of gold and green
Shimmering in all their glory.

In The City

I sit alone in a room,
As my heart sinks slowly to the floor.
I stare through the greasy window,
Into the dark of night,
The mass of lights shifting, swirling,
With each leaden breath.

I sit in silence and watch the street,
Squirming and writhing with noise and bustle,
Their grim iron faces, chained to joyless lives.
In a furnace of hatred and confusion
They chatter and scuttle like frenzied insects,
Hemmed in by sober blocks of grey, cold steel.

Bastions` of the urban life,
We are dulled and smooth at the edges:
Bound to the grime and filfth, that is the city
By an addiction all powerful -
A drug so deadly potent is money.

Heartbreak

I cannot give and I cannot receive.
I feel like a tree
With all its branches hacked off;
Inside my emotions are swimming
In all directions,
With no way to get out.
How I wish I could forget.

Mother Earth

I sit, like a frightened child
And watch in helpless frustration
As that aged, homely face
Crumbles into dust and bone.

And even as she bleeds,
I cut her further still
And clutch her to me
As I carve out more injuries.

Sometimes I'll cry and mourn
For Mother Earth,
Though her back is broken
She still carries our dead weight.

For as she silently and forgiving,
Bares her wounds, we wound ourselves
And as we await her passing
So too do we await our own.

God Bless America

This place is sinking to its knees,
Bums callin' "won't y'all help me please".
While trees and critters are slowly dyin'
I don't see no oil men cryin'.
And those Southern boys won't like your face,
If your coming from the Negro race;
Where kids 'll shoot you for a dime
To subsidise their thin white lines.
And the Lord above will cleanse the nation
For a healthy cash donation;
I take a peek out the door and see
A whole lotta crazies looking back at me.

Language Of Silence

Pupils wide open,
Filled with tremors
And shuddering to the core;
Hot panted breath
Shakes the air between us
In perfect rhythm.

The secreted smile,
A delicate finger touch
Light as insect wings,
Barely perceptible,
Yet dangerously close,
Fuses us in silence.

London

The lazy willows sway in unison
As a warming breeze rushes through the park
While the lunchtime sunbathers lie
In still, brown indolence
And the tourists' cameras click
Towards Horse Guard's Parade.

The Mall, lined with gaudy Americans,
Lush green poplars and flags,
Steams in the blazing heat;
As the taxis and cars squabble like children
For a few feet of tarmac,
Pushing and screaming all the way.

And the pavements of Knightsbridge
Whimper for one moment's mercy
Under the endless weight of rabid shoppers
That stumble about like a herd of cows,
Choked in a lead smoke atmosphere
With hands clutching at their hoards.

In Hyde Park a tramp burns slowly,
Motionless in a drunken stouper,
His dirty skin baked hard
And his sunken eyes, open but surpassing
The panting joggers that pass him by,
Flushed and cloaked in sweat.

Tonight he will sleep alone
In a subway or deserted backstreet.
While society couples dine and dance
Into the early hours,
His scrawny back will grow cold as steel,
His tired blood run cold.

And tomorrow the sun will rise
Over the shining city,
Floating on a seething pool
That bubbles below the surface
And slowly seeps through the glitz
Of good old London Town.

Adam Dunlea

Adam Dunlea grew up just outside Tralee, Co. Kerry and moved to Gorey, Co. Wexford in 1998. Always he has been inspired by the Darker side of Music, Poetry, Stories and Art. His inspiration as a poet comes from Pagan Celtic/Norse Mythology and the sheer Purity of Nature. Adam's poetry is featured on poetry.com.

All his poems reflect in one way or the other the meaning of Love, Sorrow or Hate. All that he seems to believe are intertwined in the concept of the Human/Animal Psyche. "For Life is Death and Death Life, like the absence of a Dream within a Deep slumber."

A Deep Sorrow Floats
Upon the Night Wind

A Deep Sorrow Floats Upon the Night Wind's Rage
As the Moon Reveals a Path Beyond the Shadow
Through Scourge and Flame, Blade and Blood
This is Untamed Fury that Burns in the Darkness Bright
There is and will Forever be no Hope to cleanse the Earth of its
Suffering
For The Four Storms of Hate Rage upon this Land
And Seas of Blood will Flow over the Mountains High
And The Forest's Trees will Rot and Crumble
For it is Men that Shall Destroy all that was once Beautiful.

When Shadow Falls

When Dusk has Fallen upon the Earth
The Moon Embraces the Dark in Perpetual Rapture
And All that was Once under the Sun's Glare
Has Fallen into Shadow
From Deep Within the Enchanted Forest,
I hear the Echoes of Trees Whisper upon the Wind
And I see the Flaming Eyes of a Wolf within the Stars,
Upon the River's Reflection.

When All is Lost

So Cold
Is the Eternal Silence of Echoes
For All Darkness Wanders In Death
And in this Death of Satisfaction
Where worries Escape and No Tears are shed
Where Sorrows and Melancholy are released
When All is Pure
When All is Black
When All is Dead
When All is Lost.

Stolen Freedom

Look beyond the Mists
Through the Blistering cold
A Dark Tale of Torture
All Time grows old
But to Lose all that was Beautiful
A Soft spoken Word of heritage
And Having to Hide our Purity
Tearful she has become
And will now Forever be
For her tears fill our Lakes
And Her Breasts are the Mountains
Her Heart still beats within the Land
Bound by Chains of Deceit
But Her Soul Rests in the Hearts of All that are True
All that Mourn our Loss
All that seek Vengeance
But it is far too late

Lost Hope, Lost Wisdom
Stolen Freedom.

Skies That Wept Once More

As The Black Mists Rise
Far Beyond The Hollow Hills
The Ravens Circle
Within a Dying Sky.
All that Once Was
Is Forgotten and Lost in Time
As the Past Arrives Once More
Under the Sorrow of the Moon.

Tears of Blood
Fell from the Sky
Upon the Cursed Earth Below
Sickening Screams, of Agony
From Deep Within the Forests Old
The Moon is Full
And the Wolves have Gathered
Their Eyes Ablaze Between the Trees

The Northern Wind
Whispers Secrets through the Trees
Of Realms In Darkness
Now
We Burn the Leaves Before the Frost
And Take the Fallen Lambs
For Fires Grow Deep Inside
And Burns within our Hearts.

Of Wolf and Eternal Thirst

Taken in Dreams and showed the Light
As Dark as Lunar Death
All alone and Silent
Except for the Wolves,
Howling at the passing of another Death
The Unknown Screams were Everywhere
Echoing, getting more and more Faint
But it never stopped, it Never stops
Sounding like sheer savage torture
It was Captivating
Like the sweet, sweet sound
Of an Infant Death Rattle
Luring me deeper and deeper in its Depths
So Dark, So Sorrowful
But it was Beautiful
The smell of the forest filled my lungs and my heart,
A fell Scent of fresh Blood was on the air
It tickled my nostrils
And played Havoc with my growing Hunger,
But also my thirst was ever Increasing
I did not know who or what I was searching for
But I knew I would find it
A draft of Icy Wind swept the side of my face
And as my eyes had adjusted to the Night
I could see an Entrance to a Cave on my Left
Hollow and Extremely Dark, I wandered inside.
The Sound of trickling water seemed to be getting louder
So I Continued to follow the Path
There was Death in this Chasm
Stale and Old
Its Fragrance Engulfed me
But it was Beautiful.

For All Light Shall Fade

When Once I had wandered through the Trees
Of Darkness and Shadow with a Sorrowful Breeze
Crestfallen was I of his Death
As my Father released his Final Breath
On the side of my Face where his soul had Demised
Into my Ear he left a sweet Cry
"For this wound I have left is yours to mend
As the Demons of South shall bring fourth the end
So seek the Satyrs of Deep Forests Old
For there Music the Cure, as the Legend once told"
Now I am here within the Glen
Of Satyrs and Oaks, without any Men

"Your Mind is Full" a voice said to me
"Of Hatred for the Blood of your Enemy"
Who goes there, I said in a startled air
But the Satyr was sat upon his chair
Join me I said to the little Drunk Oaf
A Bottle in hand as he gnawed on a Loaf
"For I do not want or wish to Fight
Around Trees of Green nor Realms of Ice.
But to sit on my Stool of long Dead Wood
Because this the Land where my Fathers Stood"

Alas I said to the Cowering Flee
Do you not wish this Earth to be Finally Free
"For I will Be Dead in a couple of Years
And no one will Mourn or Shed any Tears"
For that is not the Point of the Essence of Being.

Now get up and journey the ice Mountains with me
"On Frosted Mountains where Ice-winds Blow
I would Freeze and Die far beneath the Snow.
And the Wolves have Teeth as strong as Stone
They will rip me up and Grind my Bones
Of what you ask and what you seek
My Legs are now worn and I have grown Meek"

Surrounded by Satyrs at once I had been
Frightened and weak like a Horrible Dream.
So when did the Darkness Consume your Souls
You Cowards, you swine's crawl back to your holes
"Though we are small, you must not mock
For you are a Sheep, without its Flock."

Under the Shade of an Oak

Speak to me my Oaken Brother
Of all that Wounds your thoughts
People Lie, and Spirits Die
But Forever the Moon shall Guide

Within your roots, you can feel this Hate
As Darkness is your Father
And you will see, what will be
For the Wrath has come at Last

But is this what you craved before
A world that has lost its meaning
The Storms Benight the woeful Winds
But this Darkness has pure Feeling.

Dead and Gone

When once we walked upon this earth
So proud, so free were we
To see the stars, to see the sun
To behold the beautiful sea
But now all has changed
Life has taken a diverse path
Nature stands but not like once
Bearing a Sorrowful Glance
For all I see are the Dying trees
And Forest paths no more
But concrete slabs upon this land
No longer the owls shall soar
When all of this has ended
When we have become but dust
This land once pure
This land once free
A land of forgotten trust.

The Throne

Within a Sky of restlessness
Over Forests wide
You can feel the Moons presence
And hear the Winters Cry

For Dusk doth spawn the Shadow
Light, it has no name
The Beauty of the Dark
Within the Nights Embrace

Howl beneath the Silvered Moon
With fury in your Heart
Claim the Higher Throne
And seek the Dying Souls

For all that Died, now withered
Under a cloven hoof
The Trees did fall, the winds did Call
A Blood caresses All.

Geraldine Moorkens Byrne

Poet, and Musician from Dublin Ireland: born 1968, graduated UCD 1989, postgrad COCR 1990. She is Editor/Founding Editor of the Pagan Poetry Pages www.paganpoetrypages.com. Her published works include Bealtine (Jane Raeburn Anthology The Pagan Muse) Irish Cowboys (Prairie Poetry, July 2004) Dowsing (The Digest, The American Society of Dowsers) The Homecoming (Prairie Poetry, June 2006) among others: several pieces including Bealtine have been performed by groups as both theatrical and "ritual" performance.

Cliona by the Shore

I let myself in
with the key of the kings and
wrapped red ribbons
around my poor head.
'I thought you were dead' said
my mother.

I fired up at this and she waved me aside
'I merely remark' was her only reply

I heard on the news that the Temple had fallen.
I am aghast at their simple faith
And men search their words
For slivers of meanings
shards and remnants
of a truth they will hate
'you came home too late', says my mother

The debt I repaid is burning a hole in my pocket
For the cruelty of martyrs is mercy.

The wet grass smelt sweetly
Giving me courage
I willfully left there
and drove to the ocean
but none of the fishermen
put out to sea.
'Are you leaving me? ' asks my mother

I smiled in return and released her to fade.
For I am the prophet of beauty decayed.

We dwell by the shore now
And bless the white thimble
The rue grows around us
like weeds on a grave and the favour still warms us
in cottage or cave
'We'll save the world later', my wise mother says.

Lower Me Not

Lower me not,
into a crimson mouthed coffin
under mahogony covers
a secret tucked away
Lower me not
into damp clay
weighted down
by marble grey

Set me ablaze
set me free
set me flying
like a dying comet.
Across the sky
fling me, swing me,
let the wind kiss me
set me spiralling in flaming arcs.

float me away
a petalled offering
on a river of spices
through red dusty land
or rip me, espose me
the bare bones of me
speadeagled on a table rock
part of the raven, or the wolf

Lower me not,
leave me not
forget me not
let me leave you
let me depart
let me be freedom
and new life
and new dawns.

Death of the Hero

One note rising on the wind:
piper play, the lament is called for:
lower him down and softly keen
Cu Chulainn's going to his rest.

Lady Emer cry farewell
the man is bruised and broken
no token of your love will now
redeem Cu Chulainn from the grave.

hang your heads, o noble beasts
hounds of Ulster ye are bereft
no master now, for he is slain
there's is no more Cu Chulainn

men of Ulster faint and ill
bestir your voices in his name
his fame should raise you from your cots
Cu Chulainn cannot from the grave.

O grey world, no music now
no gay troop, no feasts or feis
dash the cup from kingly hands
Cu Chulainn cannot longer drink

You could not face the man in life
you feared to face him as he died
O men of munster hang your head
Cu Chulainn beat you all at last

Stand back, hang back and let
the birds of war attend his grave
only they can follow now
Cu Chulainn the hero as he goes.

Night Chorus

Across the last plains
under leaden skies,
the ground peat-brown beneath;
Turf cutters pausing to point
at the summers last black-breasted flight,
across the dark eddies and whirlpools,
the silver line of the river beneath;
Over the wild heathers of the stone hills
from the Cairns of the west
to the graves of the silent east.
A black sunset, the death of a new day remarked.

Shrill and defiant in calling
the passage of the long evening mourned.
The gravel paths of the interlopers,
darkened by the cloud of dark wings,
stirred by the shadow of the future.
The reminder that death precedes life,
The smoke of the fires rising slowly;
the wheel of the wing on the turn.
The veil drawing over the midlands,
the song of the night slowly silenced,
the call of the dusk borne away.

On the South Side of the Lake

Low cries of heron; curlew calls and circles.
In the chill air
I shiver, stamp the cold earth, hug goose-fleshed arms against
the damp
and smell the evening air of grass and turf
and just a little, smoke.

There are echoes on the air, faint calls from the other side;
carried by
the still lake water,
and whispered back and forwards through the reeds.
Above the lapping water of the south shore, is heard
The easy good humour of parents, bringing in the young to tea
And as they fade away I listen to the distant lowing of the herds
and the goodnight calls of the homebound rooks.

The day has been mild, late September's warmth and damp, with
darkly swaying trees
poised on the brink of Autumn, hinting at the pageantry to come.
Now at dusk the swallows flirt in twilight, swoop and fall against
the blue-black
rain-clouds: by morning, there will be pools among the rocks:
lakes in miniature, with waterfalls and estuaries and sailing boats
of bark and leaf.
I cast a line and light a filter-tip, the first of some thirty-odd
and huddle over the glowing end as though it were the campfire.
Perverse it may seem, but I feel warmer. Brave again, I cast again;
I watch each ripple and hope.

How dark the water now, like mirrored glass, polished to an onyx-like gleam.
The evening speeds away towards the night, bringing with it all the hunted rustles
and sudden starts, the death and lust of dark, and the agitated rising of the prey
against the thrust and dart of feathered fly, the tautened line and I, with racing heart and quickened breath, measure out the seconds of the fight and stumble, crash and shake
'til at last I see, a silvered panting form against the net. I sit and smoke and proudly guess
the weight and length and is it not the king of trout, to be landed by a woman's hand?

There are no witnesses on the south shore of the lake.
What humankind there is, is sitting on the sandy shore of the north, warmed and excited in a bonfire's light and have no notion nor do they care, for the heroic victory of the lonely angler.
I share a moment's wild excitement with my prize and then, with a whispered prayer,
gently free him from the net and ease him, with my love,
back into the waiting embrace of the lake.

Irish Cowboys

The wild west for us
was never the stone walls
and fragments of land between them
the ragged, wild, bog-spawned
west of Ireland
It was a topography, a dialect, a code
as familiar as our parents
or our national tongue
gleaned from Television, old movies
dog-eared paperbacks.
We were born in Dublin
but we all, each one,
roamed the wild praries
hunting buffalo in our souls
spat tobaccy and smoked Marlborough
walked bowlegged - howdy pardner -
or grim and gimlet-eyed, we eyed the
scorching sun
talking in monosyllabic knowing exchanges
about drought, and cattle dying, and crops failing
thwarted in our childish hearts by
near incessant rain
and insolent verdant green.

Saving Sylvie

I was restored by the sight of her
my bustling nursing Sylvie with long smiles,
and I told her so.
She shook her head, still smiling.

I am the last patient in a ward
of ten; the others have been cured
and moved on, to families
and welcomes home.
I am the death head's at the feast.
No wonder Sylvie looks so glum.

If I weren't here the rows of
starch and snow would be unbroken.
I would hold court on the balcony
be wheeled ceremoniously, one last time
to doctors' jokes and nurses' smiles.
I would if I could but I won't, you know.
I stay here just to spite you, Sylvie.

I hear they are remodelling the ward
where will they put me, I wonder?
In my darker nights I fantasise.
I am in a broom closet,
just me and the shelves
and Sylvie comes to pick up some bedlinen
and winks, woman to woman.

I am in the garden,
overgrown with ivy,
a living statue, a grey memorial
Comes my doctor with a bouquet
and behind her with a wreath,
the ever hopeful Sylvie
and she sighs, to see the empty line
on the headstone she donated.

In the bright day, I think
I may have misjudged her. I
love her even; like I love
the nectar in these tubes.
Ah, I am restored by the sight of her
galled, and reminded of my decreasing
and I told her so.
She just shook her head, still smiling.

Secrets of the Dead

When I couldn't bear it anymore
the nurse pointed to the glass door
and said:
the grounds are lovely
at this time of year.
I didn't like to tell her
I was dying for a cigarette;
there were quite a few inside,
gutted from the same.

I found a bench, private on a gravel walk
and tried to breath and inhale
all at once. I saw an old man eying me
greedily following each smoky tendril;
Jaysus, I could taste that, he whispered
and I nearly offered him one.
But the nurse stood sentinel on my manners.

Pleasantries suspended, down he sat;
flannel under duffle; woollen hat.
It's not the illness that I mind, he said
it's the dying; and he choked and wheezed
with mirth, gallows humour being in fashion here.

D'ya know what, he said, I hate the thought of them ones
pawing through my private things.
I left a letter in my bedside drawer-
I wish I'd burned it long ago. They'll
see my dirty underwear; What will they think
of the magazines? I could weep, he confided,
I'll die of the embarrassment;
this set him off again, asthmatic chuckling.

We were driven back inside with the rain;
I took up my accustomed place again
and tried to think of clever things to say
and visiting time dragged on -

while I made a mental inventory of
underwear and poetry and love letters
and tampons and diet sheets and tried
to calculate how fast they'd burn.

Territory

First
was the spear shaft
spiked in my soft flesh
with anger and with fear
and I first heard the word
'mine'

after were many spikes
cranogs and fences,
ramparts and causeways
pinpricks that tore
perforated the completeness
of my soul
and many voices shouted
'mine'

soon after
deep scars
gashes across the face of me
a million hands all grabbing
all tearing
all shouting
'mine'

All using part of me
a sacred communion
throwing me like offal to pigs
drawing lines through my
energy
all building boundaries
all enslaving me
all claiming me,
'mine'

I contemplate
spinning out of orbit
into the ice-cold rind of space
into the red-heat of a burning sun
into the wasteland of eternity
and when their shouts have silenced
point at the endlessness of time
and tell them
'mine'

Snow in Dublin

You can keep your snow-capped mountains
I can pass
on fields of virgin white.
The real power of snow is seen
on chimney stacks and pavements,
perfection silhouetted against a city skyline.
Ice on the locks
of the Canal;
Prim herbaceous borders
flaunting feather boas of powdered frost
sequined like housewives at christmas.
Children freed from board and desk
run amok. Good oldfashioned amok.
There are no smells to rival
your neighbour's breakfast
cooking on a snowy morning.
Skies of leaden foreboding,
offset by central heating and
curried chips.
The fleeting pathos of a snow day
the knife-edge balance of work and
roads too snowbound for traffic
O! the thrill.
You can keep vistas of grandeur
nothing beats the slow and stately grace
of the 46A sailing past, unable to stop
on brakes too far gone for snowy roads.

Wil Kinghan

Wil is a Shamanic Practitioner in the native Celtic traditions and has been exploring the Irish and North European mysteries since childhood when, aged 15, he bought a book on Runes.

He has explored many diverse paths of magic and spirituality and is currently working in the mysteries of Merlin and is training as a bard with the Order of Bards, Ovates and Druids, he is also involved in the development of native men's mysteries and rites of passage.

He believes strongly in nurturing the links between the land, ancestors and people today, and in the creation of new accessable myths to help us reforge the bridge to the world of our allies, the spirits.

His primary creative skill is as an artist and he creates ritual tools in bronze, and paintings and icons of the Celtic deities and spirits. Wil is also a qualified Counsellor and Hypnotherapist, which he feels is an important occupation in todays society given the lack of support available to people in daily life.

Tuán's song to the sons of Nemed

Across the ninth wave
Brave Nemed's fleet
Thirty times thirty pale warriors
To defeat tall Eiru's cliffs.

I, Tuán, in my stony cell
Watch, disinterested…
From my eyes, farseeking,
A new shell.

Brave stag of seven tines
Accomplished war-leader
Of the hooved hosts
In a new shape before hunters.

I will see fair Fotla's history,
Though they see me not.

Sea Spell

She plays catch with Manannan Mac Lír
Old sea god and young sea child
Blond hair like kelp
Wracked upon a roaring sea-horse
That surely bore Oisin to Tir na Óg.

I ply my boat in the shadow of rocks
Beach-combing the detritus of land
Fearing perhaps the careless beauty of my sea-nymph
Exulting in salt air and tidal pool she finds,
A piece of driftwood carved with runes…
To summon again the long ships from the sunken lands.

Vile

Is there no end to vile requests
24 hours it might take me,
To do as you ask!
I stare into the faces of my companions
And realise that they are going home!
They pledge my labour, seemingly indifferent
840 megabytes, I think in dismay
Envisioning grey boxes aflame!
"We need them for the morning…"
The grey man in the grey suit looks at me
Eyes like vacant pools
Devoid of understanding, and I wonder…
Does he have a soul?
And has he any fucking home to go to!

Father

Across the circles of time
Grieving still,
But yet not grieving.
Awash on the shoreline
The driftwood bobs
In and out on the swell.
Water flashes,
Rushes out away from me
Sending that little log
Further away across a sea of time,
'Till I no longer even remember it...
But feel deprived
Of it's passing.
And knowing...
That I should have befriended that lonely wood!
Fellow traveller
Speck of the ocean...
Who knows when
Our ships may pass again.

After

Dead emptyness haunts the streets
A carrion crow picks at dead bones
Birch trees sway,
Gently tingling breeze
A crecent moon rises, 'neath
The chevron flight of birds.
The old rusty car is a haven now
For Cat or Harvest Mouse
Once feared for crushing those clans
They find it now a home.
The hand of Man once fashioned these towers
Interesting jigsaws
Artistic, majestic decay...
Crumbling concrete and drip-drip metal.
A tangle of wires falls
A mute cobweb hung about
Silent monitors.
A carpet of moss furrs the long-dead keyboards
And fading signs
How long will it take for them to fade away?
Only time knows
And he is endless.
Nobody hurries now on the silent streets
Peace now in the empty stations
Hush world! There is nobody here
To sweat
Or stress
Or trouble your quiet creatures...
All is as it was meant to be.

Rumours

Rumours abound!
From people who are no-names
Vicious lies
Bred in the darkness
"You know who your friends are!", they say...
When you find unspoken words
That draw pictures of
Scurrilous deeds!
But I am used to the outside
Forever apart,
Among those not approved of...
Or thought dangerous...
A canvas,
Suitably mysterious
For those more rightious
To project their fantasies!

None of it is true of course,
The reality is pedestrian
And dull...
And oh so viciously normal!

The Magus

The pebble beach
Pockmarked by sea-wrack
Precious stones
And wood for carving signs.
The Great Sea abides…
Binah, Marah!
With force-plumed sea horses
To assault the land.
For a long time lost, I once again
Feel alive!
Once more the Magus I command the waves
They grow fierce and strong
Under my Will
And I feel once more the power
For a time I had forgotten
It's abilty to thrill!

Jack in the Green

Jack in the Green,
Jack in the Green
Here is a face
That might never be seen.

From font to forest
To gable-end,
In the crook in the road
Waits Uriel's friend.

On the tower and the summit
With Michael's sword,
In the ditch and the wallow
With Our Lady's furrow.

Both Fire and Frost
He'll be in-between...
Oh Jack in the Green,
Jack in the Green.

Epona

They invoke you from the hills
Goddess of white horses...
Sweet fleet footed Night-mare
Deadly wanderer of fretful dreaming.

The dew left in your wake is poison
Or Grail-worthy elixir,
Combed from your sides
On devil-chased night rides.

Epona, you loom large
In the enchanted isle,
And further still, as Red Macha...
Black, red, white are your colours,
Dark, full and crecent, riding
The long mile paths...
To harry long forgotton legions.

The Adze-head that cried like a deer

'Tis spoken of with awe -
When the Tealceann enchanted his flock
To escape capture
In the shape of a deer.

There was not a power (within the land)
That he did not invoke!
To make his spell
Of the beguiling deer-shape.

Would the son of the unspoiled mother
Stoop to such a trick?
Laughed the scalds and poets,
Rather that the cup be taken from him!

Was it 3 days then, O Patrick,
Sojourner without man-shape?
What recalled you to us but a Christian power,
What took you hence but a Pagan one!

Toddy Kennedy

Toddy Kennedy began his dying the moment of his birth in 1963. Still alive at time of going to press. He has spent the last 25 years often as a bricklayer, more frequently as an unofficial and unpaid taster of stout. His first book of poetry titled "Introduction", was published by Electric Publications in Oct. 2004. He regards himself as an Arklowman.

A View From Barnisky

An October sky from where mortals lie
To their eternal peace,
Now understanding,
That the spark shall never cease.
Dead! To just the living,
Endless in their grave,
We know that we are immortal,
To stand at heavens portal,
For our God will call the chosen
In their time to gather hay,
For we shall never
Know the moment,
We won't see the light of day.

Even Barmen Retire

Like comrades standing
Cannons dry
In congregation gather by
This place of lore
And story told
In credit to your person fold
With fond abandon
Cluster near
To drink a toast to one so dear
When all the world
To patience tries
He shoots the breeze
Who's to wonder why?

Fresh Water Fishing

There will be another lake in Cavan
When its time to say goodbye,
It will be hard to keep the tears
From welling in my eye,
However from all peaks I'll scan
Wherever I might make a stand,
Be it on some far flung
Foreign place
Where no man stood
To see the beauty of your face,
And will condemn the very
Error of my days
That led me once to Cavan town,
And the parting of the ways.

Full Moon

Our time and turn
Is coming soon
Waylaid by the shadow
Of a perfect moon,
Undaunted by perceptions
Slow to take my leave
From my berth
Upon the north beach,
I know you know
That I believe
Tomorrow while it starts
To wane,
There will still be elements
Of pain,
Yet when the lunar circle
Reappears,
We shall amble carelessly
Bereft of tears.

June 6th

The guns fell silent
One by one,
As did countless
Millions more.
They stood in line
To genuflect,
And marched away
To war.
The yanks are in
The firing line,
But yet they're not
In Palestine.
A new world order
Holds its breath,
Their lesser fears
Align themselves with death.
"Freedom" cries the Chechen,
"Freedom" cries the Basques,
Freedom cried the dead and maimed,
The consequence
Of the gruesome tasks.
"Freedom is the oxygen of my soul"
Cried Moshe Dyan,
The great, the bloody great,
And the warmonger that's man.

Safely in The Arms of Tomorrows Thoughts

Only saw the light,
When your shadow
Faded temporally
Out of sight,
Waded knee deep
Into the passions
Which I knew were there,
But put on hold
Because of you,
Accept that life deals fate
To those who know
And those who wait,
Strip veneer off old and
Worn out frames of mind
To meet myself in passing,
And care less
To look behind.

Skyline

My happiness knows yet no horizons
But those you have shown me
Was I to fall from favour?
From your grace
On swallow's wings I'd fly
To lay my beating soul
With you
Its rightful place.

So...You're Back!

You are the conclusion,
Of my every day,
My Christmas tree in June,
My star chart
Through the Milky Way,
My foothold on the Moon,
My drop of rain
On dusty roads,
My bond with missing links,
My helper with the heavy loads,
I fear you may be jinxed.

Unfinished Sympathy

I have felt the loneliness of loss,
Exuberant joy in the knowing
That what was lost
Was love
And now this, what is this
Is it hate?
For I am certain
Of its all consuming rage
The time, which spent on other things
Than this
Is sleeping, yet dreaming of days
Of halcyon days
Within your rapture
Perhaps this is what love is all about
A passion which commands
A total spell
The view of Heaven from the gates of Hell.

Strolling

Thought I'd saunter
While the night remains
Cold comfort
Nothing new
Found myself in judgement
Of the aching
Had not allowed for you
To break the stillness
The reflection, the questions
'cross the sea
Alone, but never on my own
From the depths, the mystery
Of where I've found contentment
The will to strive for more.

The Bowsie

Paused to redirect attention from
The person whom I'd come to be,
Stood back and looked in vain,
For what was left of me
Searched the often
Scoured the frequent,
Hit on all the well known haunts
With no return,
Found myself back, where
I first could feel it burn,
And prayed to unknown gods
That I would find salvation,
Defy the odds,
Not easy being a rock of sense,
While all around you
Quicksand.

Cait Branigan

Cait Branigan is Founder and Editor of Immrama Magazine and a member of the Order of Bards, Ovates and Druids. She facilitates the Full Moon Writing Circle, which seeks to enhance creative expression and poetic inspiration. Cait runs a healing practice in Wexford and teaches both in Ireland and abroad.

Epiphany

I saw here and there as she ran,
Holding aloft a blade of grass
Like some Elusinian vision,
That she was free.
Tasting all, experiencing all,
She bellowed her beauty
With full lungs.
She is no shrinking violet
Who shies from her senses.
Her eyes are of Hawk,
Spotting in obscurity
The key to her delight.
She is Sovereign unto
Herself, a blazing light
In the darkness of life's
Great Womb Cauldron.
And I see her, with her blade
Of grass, her epiphany, her
Mystery. I see my child
In full splendour – a child
Of the Great Goddess.

Of the Sorrows

The innocent bliss and glow of blood
In cheek. Dark as the Raven whose
Blood soaks the snow. You are more
Wonderous to me than the grains in the
Basket, for you are the sacred embodiment
Of colour. And I pine for you now.
And I call out your name.
Naoise, Naoise – treading the waves
Away from your death.
Shall I comb out my hair for the
Two unholy rams? I am the All-seeing
Most sacred eye. I have seen my own
Death in the goblet of wine. The heroes
Are spoiled with idolatry. Where have I gone?
I am lost to myself and alone.

Sea-Struck

The sea spreads wide on open thigh
Breast exposed, teasing the waves
As sun kissed the foam of the sea mares.
Manannan looks on in wonder at
This female figure frolicking on a cold
Windy day. What care is there when
Life pushes into the world, manifesting,
Creating, unfurling?
The sky, so vast, hung with clouds
Of warm moisture like my lips.
They threaten a downpour swearing
To be true, to nourish this, your
Earth. Where sea and sky co-mingle
There is dappling of mystic hooves
On wave. Manannan looks on
In wonder at thigh and breast and
Divine Freedom.

Rain

I can hear the rain, or at least
What remains of its odious
Outpouring. Battering my window,
Shouting unmercilessly, "Hear me!
See me!" I heard, I saw
But the road winced at the
Ferocity. Swiping blindly at
This emotional flood.
"Why? Why? Why?"
I peer closer, the light diffused
By a thousand passionate tears.
Relentless, it pours.
Relentless, I drive.
Until at last, it heaves no
More under the sobbing clouds.
The rains slows. The rain clears.
From behind the clouds, the
Moon emerges, glorious.

Breath of Life

Fight chest and lungs
Purging mucuous of
Memories lost.
Breath ragged,
Wheezing, coughing
It through.

Screaming lungs.
Drowning lungs.
Lips blue.
Dark curtains.
Old doorways
To go through.

Red tent
Powerfully present.
Raven ferryman
Patiently waiting.
Breath easier
Deeply tranced.

Slowly returning.
Oars propelling,
Guides waiting.
Memories.
Memories.
Memories real.
Memories lost.

Tears

I am enchanted by your tears.
Singing into vision, the joy that
Brings the water to your eyes.
What lost child is awed by the
Meanderings of a child's play?

What pain is buried like a
Chest, a buried treasure
Waiting to be found so laughter
And the graceful play will
Be the experience, not the Metaphor.

Tears 2

She cried when she saw the rain,
Though she loves the water. The heavy
Splat, splat of the drops stole her
Plans to slide into paradise for the
Day. It washed them down the
Drain like stale cabbage water.

She cried when she saw the rain
And no amount of kisses could
Soothe her suffering sobs. Each
Tear a frustrated disappointment
As the clouds opened on top of her,
Myriad pools of boredom.

Rose

The soft petal with rosy hue
Is my gift to you. Shall you
Plunder it with rough touch or
Shll you hold and caress it
With intent and knowing?
The folds of the petals each
Hold their own sweetness and
Sensation. Shall you taste
Of their juices as you savour
Its splendour? Sweetest of
Roses, red as the blood of
Clay, do you see my gift or
Your own desire manifest?

Lost Child

Somewhere on these pages, I think
She may be found. Amid all the
Noise and repulsive over-expression
She lies hidden.
Somewhere in the sadness which
Pollutes these pages I catch sight
Of her shadow – rushing into dark
Corners of simile and cliché.
Somewhere within this self-indulgence
She must still be waiting.
Waiting for someone to remember
She wishes to be found.

Eyes

There was a light, I saw it there clearly,
Shining out from water, smiling eyes.
Those eyes which have seen the divine and
Borne witness. Those eyes that have gazed
Into the deep, unfathomable pools of emotion
Seeing there the birth of wisdom.

Sitting, observing, my hands gesticulating
My mouth lending itself to allies of
Anonymous realms; aware as the quietness
Of my spirit saw, in truth, her journey
As fruitful, connected, validated. Causing
My soul to pause and wonder.

What can be seen in my eyes – these
Grey blues, reminiscent of the grey sea?
What do they reveal of my journey – a
Journey which has crashed on the rocks,
Sold me to sirens and freed my soul
From self-imposed delusions?

Again, the stillness.
Again, the stillness.

Gemma McCabe

Gemma McCabe was born in Dublin but now lives in county Wexford. Gemma is a teacher and a counselor, she also works as a music therapist.

Expression

Harness it. Come One. Come One.
Let's get to it.
It started. It happened.
I saw it all clear and raw.
Me, the evolution.
The dream and the goal.
Blessed by a certain Vision.
Of the desire within.
Untouched by tongue.
And so it shall remain.

Beating

I fail to live, I fail.
Suchness embraces my hollow core,
And rattles my empty cage.
Where once my heart beat so free.

I sit on my perch and view from within
The dusty corners of me.
Feelings hidden far from my me.

No touch, no taste does satisfy me.
I cry, I weep and barely pray.
Emerse myself in a shady coil
Of loves untrodden dream
And pound upon my breast.

Is this my life as I see fit?
Don't I get a say in my hearts last trip?
To the loves anguished and soul forlorn apartment;
My broken heart's last abode.

I beat my drum slowly and stare into it.
Eyes wide gazing.
No flights no flit.
No flutter of eye.
No lick of lash.
Simply it and simply me.

Im ready for you, O heartless wonder.
I ache to scratch at your all.
Don't think I'll go meekly this time.
Im here to take on your all.
I'll wait you know
And if you choose to hide
I'll be here when you peep out the door.
Checking to see if I've gone
Under sea and wave
And deafened my ear to your roar.

Can you hear my rhythm?
Can you tell it's me?
Oh I'm here alright
Just wait and see.

Fighting fit and angry as Hel,
I want to hear injustice yell.
And it's cry from deep within.

Letting Go

Excellence pervails within.
Waves carry my hurt.
It glints and thunders
And I simply hear.
I paint its colour with eye.
Dip a toe into the splash it creates.
It pleases.
I hum.
And sing with full throated ease.

Connected

Shippers way and sailors delight
It's something I never thought of
Instantaneous lover's thought
Resides in melody.
It covers my memory.

And simply now
I come undone
Up front and next to none.

Poetic song
Like repeated bird
Awakes in me my love.

Wish

Flourescent kiss and
Fingers begin to tip
The dream I will to be.
We stretch our palms
And carry on.
Twisting in our real.
But with twirling eyes
And open arms
I dance to a raging sea.
I light my dreaming me.
Tell her how I want it to be.
My souls desire and fire be.

Untitled 1

Sitting still, yet trembling with tears
I died inside.
Wings purged me still
And down forever I went.
Bleakest drive right through my heart
And sharp claw blinded my soul.
All you could hear were the screams of pain
That couldn't be heard only felt.
By you.
You held me in your world
And surrounded my falling life
With the stuff of love.
I bounced upon the light of voice
And cried out my soul to your ears.
You held me in your arms.
And while you were not even here,
You cradled me gently and rocked me a lulaby.
Vulnerability surrounded.
Yet you cuddled with care
Patting my hair off my tear stained cheek
Even though you were there.
Hours of tide drowning my air.
No bubble of hope gave me a chance.
Except for you travelling here.
You know you saved my life.
You know you have delivered me
From my very own birth.
Love has turned and scorched me pure.
I would be a cinder
Had you not been sure for me.
And there on bended knee.
Aching inside to guide me.
Me. Through the fiercest of storms.
You carried me safe to Home.
Safe.

In your arms I faded away.
And became the tops of the trees.
You made me remember the leaves.
Can you know the power you gave
In your arms you banished my grave.
Trust that I will know,
The amount of good in soul,
That has brought you to my world,
That cradles and rocks my world.

Empty

All might be known
And all might be lost.
Duality is forever riding me.
Wipped and tormented into distraction
Until all else tumbles down into my ache.

And there I pause and don't breathe.
Barely. And empty within.
Empty.
I move eyes and wait.
Small air.
Nothing.
Double up and twist on my side.

I scratch at my pain and howl.
Nothing in me for months now.
Hope lost as never before.
Expectations have flown and
Head to head with death
I consider.

Untitled 2

Your words cast spells upon my heart.
So much so my mind is full.
Enchantment.
It stirs upon my pen.
And quickens the womb within.
And letting go of glass so clear,
I pull you close and exhale fear.

Belief within and out of cause.
I sent that wish and pushed out love.

In this night of racing mind
When I could wake to all of that
Which pulses my air and twirls my pen,
My eyes wont rest until rhyme has spun.

Cascading flow and sudden surprise,
The night of sound and roar outside
I blink and hear the poems arise
And curse you for keeping me awake!
I'd love to finish this make.
I've been hoping all words would asleep.
Yet instead I am banished from peep!

This paper will soak up the wet
From not having loved you thus yet.
I'll ride to you chancing my fall
I'll hide from you only a small.

Pulse bitten tender
And smother this fright.
Tell me you love me and
End all my fight.
Place hand around my shivering waist.
Blink tears away from my pleasures disgrace.

Amen to this blessing.
Adieu to your hurt.
Come for this earth-shattering mindset-full love.

Take me, don't leave me
I'll promise inside.
Pause-break, don't hope for
That less than Divine.

Away from our blankets
Afar from the Sea
Above from not made
This most treasure of thee.

Loving I owe you
Leaving my heart.
Loosing adore you
To place of thou art.

Also available from Electric Publications...